C000102220

Islamic Laws of
Expiation
(al-Kaffarat)

ISLAMIC LAWS OF
Expiation
(al-Kaffarat)

According to the rulings of Grand Ayatullah
al-Sayyid Ali al-Husseini al-Sistani

The most important Islamic laws about expiation for
breaking a fast during the month of Ramadan,
the non-fulfillment of a vow, breaking an oath,
physical assault (severe hitting), abortion, and more

I.M.A.M.

IMAM MAHDI ASSOCIATION OF MARJAEYA

Imam Mahdi Association of Marjaeya, Dearborn,
MI 48124, www.imam-us.org
© 2018 by Imam Mahdi Association of Marjaeya
All rights reserved. Published 2018.
Printed in the United States of America

ISBN-13: 978-0-986-29516-4

Contents

Contents

I.M.A.M.'s Foreword

In the name of Almighty Allah

May Allah shower His blessings upon
Prophet Muhammad (pbuh) and his family (p)

This booklet is part of a series of abridged and precise practical jurisprudential rules that seek to provide guidance to Muslims living in the West. The content of this booklet (and subsequent booklets) is specifically written using simplified language that can be easily understood by non-specialized readers of jurisprudential texts. The series clarifies the most important issues of applied Islamic practice (i.e., Islamic laws) facing our youth who are living and growing up in the West and who have reached the age at which they are responsible for performing and fulfilling their religious duties. These Islamic laws are written in accordance with the edicts (*fatwas*) of the top religious authority of the Shia sect, His Eminence Grand Ayatullah Ali al-Sistani (may God prolong his life). They are specifically derived from his books *Minhaj al-salihin* and *Al-taliqah ala al-urwah al-wuthqa* and what has been published on the official website of the Office of His Eminence in the Holy City of Najaf, Iraq.

This booklet focuses on the Islamic laws of expiation (*kaffarat*) for several reasons, most importantly for the following three reasons.

THE INFORMATION, RESOURCES, AND DETAILS OF THE
subject of expiation are scattered in the traditional
books of jurisprudence (*fiqh*)—like those on Islamic
laws and other books of religious edicts written by
jurists. Therefore, it is often difficult for those who are
reaching or have reached the age of Islamic puberty[i]
and hence are responsible to perform their religious
duties, to access these various jurisprudence books and
get answers to their questions and resolutions to their
issues in a detailed, appropriate, and correct way. As such,
the goal of collecting, simplifying, and organizing these
rules into a single booklet is to provide a reference that
is easily understood and readily accessible.

ACTS OF EXPIATION ARE AMONG THE MOST CHALLENGING
and problematic issues facing the members of our
communities because either people do not know about
them, misunderstand their rules, or are ignorant about
their application. People frequently feel burdened by
the sinful acts they have committed and need to seek
forgiveness and purify themselves through expiation
in addition to commonly used invocations like *istighfar*.
Therefore, the system of expiation is designed by God
to forgive and purify His worshippers who have
committed a wrongful act due to their ignorance or
negligence or because they listened to evil Satanic
whispers. So, it is one of the means through which God
Almighty shows His Mercy towards His slaves who wish
to seek forgiveness and ask for repentance for what
they missed of their obligatory acts of worship or as a
worldly penalty (as opposed to the next world) for
committing a *haram* (sinful) act.

> *Therefore, the system of expiation is designed by God to forgive and purify His worshippers who have committed a wrongful act due to their ignorance or negligence or because they listened to evil Satanic whispers.*

WE WANT TO COMPILE A PRELIMINARY RESOURCE THAT describes the wisdom behind an expiation system and the reason for having it in Islam. On the one hand, the goal is to raise the level of general knowledge of our community members and on the other to clarify the misconceptions or answer the questions that are raised due to commonly encountered circumstances.

The contents of this booklet are as follows:

- An introduction to expiation that defines and explains the importance of the system of penalties (as an act of worship) and reform in Islam

- Types of expiation that may be challenging or problematic for worshippers to implement with a statement about each type and its related duties

- Special subjects related to expiation such as abortion, which continues to be one of the most problematic issues in today's world and thus needs to be addressed in some detail

- A section titled "addendum" that includes the discussion of jurists and what they have said about occasional issues or what has been written about edicts that were not mentioned in traditional books of Islamic laws—for example, hitting children

- A section on performing expiation that provides details on how a Muslim should fulfill the process and achieve confidence in completing it correctly. Also addressed here are different situations that may arise and how to act to ensure the proper performance of expiation in each case.

- An epilogue, which presents certain moral recommendations and guidelines concerning recommended and desirable (*mustahabb*) expiation—expiation that contributes to building a sound and pure heart in a Muslim who consciously strives to move away from the negative aspects of life and enhance their spiritual and faithful qualities.

Sayyid M.B. Kashmiri
Jurist Representative
I.M.A.M.

Acknowledgements

We would like to thank, and send our sincere appreciation to, all those who have contributed to preparing and processing the materials needed to bring this booklet to light. We specifically would like to thank everyone who has written, reviewed, edited, and published this content from among staff and volunteers who are part of this blessed association, I.M.A.M. We particularly would like to thank His Eminence Sayyid Monir al-Khabaz for his time and effort in reviewing and editing the content of this booklet. We ask God Almighty to accept this work as purely to Him for the benefit of Islam and Muslims living in the West. We ask God to let this work be a useful tool for Muslims to learn more about their religion and to try to reach the ultimate goal of a human being, which is to seek perfection.

This booklet was translated and reviewed by Brother Haidar Mazen and Dr. Haj Mehdi Saeed Hazari respectively.

I.M.A.M.

Introduction

Islam Is a Religion of Mercy, So Why Punishment?

One of the most prominent attributes of God Almighty is that He is merciful or *rahman* to everything and beneficent or *rahim* to the believers. He has provided a religion imbued with mercy through prophets and messengers who embodied God's grace perfectly. So, why does God impose punishments and obligate expiation?

Very briefly, commensurate with the size of this booklet, we say:

Whoever studies the religion of Islam objectively from all its aspects and logically and reasonably examines its true fundamental sources, the Holy Quran and the verified and accurate narrations of Prophet Muhammad and his holy household (*hadith*), will find that religion is a complete system of life. The person will definitely discover clarifications to many misconceptions and answers to questions and problems.

The penalty code is a pillar of the Islamic system that in its entirety ensures human happiness both from the perspective of personal improvement and advancement as well as preservation of societal balance. Since Islam is an integrated system comprised of many other essential codes, like those related to social and economic conduct, security and orderliness, education, public administration, and family practices, it also includes a disciplinary (punitive) system.

Yet with some deliberation and reflection, and from an objective point of view, it is clear that the code of expiation is a manifestation of divine mercy in two important ways: (1) it mitigates the spiritual deficiencies that result from personal sins, and (2) it acts as a strong deterrent against future sins.

This Islamic penal (disciplinary) system provides remedies for three types of wrongdoings, each of which has its own scope, laws, and conditions.

First: Limits (*hudud*)

The first of the transgressions are concerned with the right of God, so no one other than God has the right to change the law or pardon any human being. He says, "These are Allah's bounds, so do not transgress them, and whoever transgresses the bounds of Allah—it is they who are the wrongdoers" (Quran 2:229). These limits are known, recognized, and explicitly mentioned in the Holy Quran and the hadith such as the punishment for theft, drinking wine, adultery, homosexual relationships/acts, and others. Included in this section are the penalties for violating the general rights of God—like consciously (i.e., on purpose) breaking a fast during the month of Ramadan—as a result of which the limits of God are exceeded. Due to this transgression, a person must give/perform expiation called *kaffarah* of which they are not absolved.[ii] Expiation (kaffarah) also applies to other transgressions in this category, which are not covered in this booklet.

Second: Retribution (*qisas*) and financial reparation (*diyya*)

The second type of transgression is that which can be absolved by way of retribution[iii] or financial reparation/compensation. It relates to the actions of a person upon themselves or upon others that can be pardoned. For example, the intentional murder of a human being requires either retribution or financial reparation. Yet, besides repenting to God and seeking forgiveness from Him, Islam encourages pardon instead of retribution. God says, "But he who is pardoned some of it by his brother should be dealt with equity [*sic*], and recompense (for blood) paid with a grace. This is a concession from your Lord and a mercy" (Quran 2:178). Another example could be if someone intentionally or accidentally injures or damages another person's body part such as an eye or an ear, or breaks another's hand or leg, and so on. The same goes for abortion, which requires both a financial reparation and an expiation (kaffarah).

Third: Judicial sentences (*tazirat*)

The third of the transgressions are those that are addressed by judicial sentences. They are generally concerned with wrongdoings or sins that are not specified within particular divine limits (the first type) or absolution through retribution or a financial reparation (the second type). For this reason, they are left to the current legitimate jurist[iv] to evaluate according to the relevant circumstances and the causes and consequences of that specific wrongdoing. These judicial sentences are so numerous that they cannot all be described with written examples here. Nonetheless, a few clear examples include backbiting, bribery, betrayal, creating disturbance (*fitna*) and other transgressions that often lead to social problems and disorder, which eventually may require the intervention of the current legitimate jurist for help. The jurist will try to solve the ongoing problems by asking each party to compromise and forgive each other, otherwise he will require the person who incited the issue (i.e., committed the transgression) to be penalized in a specific way. The ensuing sentence would be carried out by the jurist himself if he is capable and has the authority to do so.

A System of Education and Rehabilitation

God's vision for human beings is different from all other creatures. God has created human beings with a pure, sound, and virtuous innate nature. Unlike the rest of

His creatures, God has given humans free will and the choice of doing good or bad in this life; this is driven by one of two opposing forces: (1) the mind and logic and (2) desires and whims. On the one hand, He has specified that those people whose minds triumph over their desires are considered superior to angels. As such, the loftiest of heights (in terms of nearness to God) to which a person can reach is described when God speaks about Prophet Muhammad (pbuh), "Then he drew nearer and nearer until he was within two bows' length or even nearer" (Quran 53:8–9). On the other hand, those whose desires triumph over their minds are considered inferior to voracious animals. About this God said, "And certainly We have created for hell many of the jinn and the men; they have hearts with which they do not understand, and they have eyes with which they do not see, and they have ears with which they do not hear; they are as cattle, no, they are more astray; these are the heedless ones" (Quran 7:179).

From this perspective, the Islamic punishment system has been created to include stringent penalties that act as a strong deterrent to keep people away from sins and preserve their pure innate nature. In addition, some will not repent and stop committing sins and forbidden acts, like abusing others and disregarding their sanctity and rights, which could lead, for example, to intentional murder. However, the penalty will cause them to think about the consequences of their actions and be deterred from contemplating subsequent wrongful acts. God has declared, "And there is life for you in (the law of) retribution, O men of understanding, that you may guard yourselves" (Quran 2:179). In other words, the Islamic punishment system in itself is the means for saving a person's life—a person who otherwise could easily be a victim of aggression or assault.

Similarly, a person who intends to break divine laws, disregarding their holiness and sanctity, like breaking a fast during the holy month of Ramadan, will then think twice before doing so. This is because that person knows that there is a severe punishment for performing that wrong act, which in this case is to fast two consecutive months for only one single day of a wrongfully missed fast. Thus, they will refrain and never think about breaking a fast. Even among people who have already committed a sin due to the power of lust triumphing over the power of reason are those who, soon after waking up, feel regret and turn back to their Lord. Hence, God the Most Merciful, says, "Surely Allah does not forgive that anything should be associated with Him, and forgives what is besides that to whomsoever He pleases; and whoever associates anything with Allah, he devises indeed a great sin" (Quran 4:48). The key to reform for these regretful people is for them to implement the right form of atonement (i.e., expiation) for their mistakes and guilt, which will then contribute to the strengthening of the deterrent force within them and initiate improvement.

This is the most nurturing system on Earth, one that promotes discipline and yet can be tolerated by every person once they examine it and understand all its aspects. This is the case because its source is the Creator of humankind Himself, who knows His people, their needs, and how to deal with their mistakes more than anyone else. As such, a person by their innate nature and pure essence is certain that (1) God exists and surrounds everything, (2) He is the most just and gracious, (3) He is the one who covers sins and wrongdoings, and (4) He is the First, the Last, the Forgiver, the Merciful, and the one who accepts the repentance of His servant. It is the very reason the sinner turns back to God, prays, and seeks forgiveness from Him no matter what their degree of faith. Ultimately, we come to realize that religion is mercy, and the system of discipline and punishment is mercy as well and certainly not a curse as it might be misunderstood.

Definition of Expiation

The word 'expiation' or *kaffarah*

The origin and root of the Arabic word is (ك ، ف ، ر) *kfr*, which is derived from كَفَرَ and means to cover, to hide, concealment, and denial.[v] The word كافر or *kafir*, which means a disbeliever (or infidel) in God, is derived from this origin. Another of its meanings is the night, whose darkness covers and hides everything, and the farmer or the planter who covers seeds with soil. God has said, "Like the example of a rain whose [resulting] plant growth pleases the tillers [*kuffar*]" (Quran 57:20).

Usage in Islamic jurisprudence

In Islamic jurisprudence and religious terminology, 'expiation' (or *kaffarah* in this case) means to cover and compensate for one's sins by giving charity or fasting. Thus, expiation of sin is considered a means of concealment and purification from sin.[vi,vii]

Types of Expiation

The topic of expiation and its details and explanations will be presented as follows:

Pre-ordained (*al-murattaba*)

- Expiation for accidental killing
- Expiation for intentionally breaking a make-up (*qada*) fast of a day of the month of Ramadan after midday

Optioned (*al-mukhayyara*)

- Expiation for intentionally breaking a fast in the holy month of Ramadan
- Expiation for nullifying an obligatory period of spiritual retreat (*itikaf*)
- Expiation for breaking a formal pledge (*ahd*)

Combined (*al-murattaba* and *al-mukhayyara*)

- Expiation for swearing to leave off intercourse with one's wife (*ilaa*)
- Expiation for breaking an oath (*yamin*)
- Expiation for breaking a vow (*nadhr*)

Designated (*al-muayyana*)

- Expiation for swearing/testifying to something (i.e., upon something sacred like God) and then committing perjury

Comprehensive (*al-jame*)

- Expiation for intentionally killing a believer

Type 1

·············◆◆◆·············

Pre-ordained (al-Murattaba) Expiation

Definition

Pre-ordained (al-murattaba) expiation is expiation that should be performed in a specific order according to one's strength and ability.[viii] Here, the required obligation is to follow the defined convention—for example, fasting two consecutive months in the case of an accidental killing. If the person is legitimately not able to fast (two consecutive months), they are then permitted to perform a specific alternative expiation, which is feeding sixty poor people.[ix] However, if the person is even not able to feed sixty poor people, then as an obligatory precaution,[x] they should fast for eighteen days along with seeking pardon from God and asking for forgiveness. If, in an extreme case, fasting is not possible at all, then the person need only to seek pardon and ask for forgiveness.

Circumstances

Pre-ordained expiation is applied in a number of cases,[xi] most importantly:

ONE: One who intentionally breaks a make-up (qada) fast of a day of the month of Ramadan after midday[1]

Any person who missed a fast(s) in the previous month of Ramadan should be diligent and make up the day(s) prior to the next month of Ramadan. If a person makes an intention to fast a make-up day and remains fasting past midday, then they should make sure to complete the fast. If this person breaks the fast deliberately after midday, expiation becomes obligatory, which for this transgression is feeding ten poor people. If the person is unable to do that, then they should fast for three days.[2]

TWO: Accidental killing

To begin, murder is one of the major sins in Islam. God has promised hellfire for the person who intentionally kills another human being and made equal and exact retribution the punishment. God has said, "And there is life for you in (the law of) retribution, O men of understanding, that you may guard yourselves" (2:179). On the other hand, accidental killing happens when

---

1. *Zawal* (midday) is the time of the noon prayer when the sun crosses the meridian. It changes during the different times of year depending on the length of day and night.

2. The original missed fast(s) will still have to be made up.

there is no intention or premeditation involved. For example, someone who is carelessly handling a weapon, like a gun, mistakenly fires and kills someone; or a person who is not ready to operate a car drives and accidentally kills a pedestrian. Perhaps another scenario might be a mother accidentally falling asleep on her breast-feeding baby causing it to suffocate and die. The expiation for such circumstances is murattaba, and, as such, a financial reparation is required since God has said, "It is not for a believer to kill a believer except (that it be) by mistake, and whosoever kills a believer by mistake, (it is ordained that) he must set free a believing slave and a compensation (blood money, i.e., diyya) be given to the deceased's family, unless they remit it. If the deceased belonged to a people at war with you and he was a believer; the freeing of a believing slave (is prescribed), and if he belonged to a people with whom you have a treaty of mutual alliance, reparation (blood money/diyya) must be paid to his family, and a believing slave must be freed. And whosoever finds this (the penance of freeing a slave) beyond his means; he must fast for two consecutive months in order to seek repentance from Allah. And Allah is Ever All-Knowing, All-Wise" (4:92).

........•◆•◆•........

Optioned (al-Mukhayyara) Expiation

Definition

Optioned (al-mukhayyara) expiation gives the person a choice of selecting one of two options, either fasting two consecutive months or feeding sixty poor people.

If a person intentionally breaks a fast of the month of Ramadan and is unable to fulfill expiation by fasting for two consecutive months, they have the option of feeding sixty poor people as expiation instead. Yet, if it is not possible for the person to fulfill either of these, they should give charity according to their means at the time. Further, if the person is even unable to do that, then they should ask for pardon and forgiveness from God understanding however that if they become capable of fulfilling expiation afterwards, then as an obligatory precaution, the expiation is due.

Al-mukhayyara expiation also applies when a person nullifies an obligatory spiritual retreat (itikaf) or breaks a pledge (ahd); and if that person is unable to fulfill either of the two expiation options, then they should fast eighteen days. Further, if the person is not even able to do that, then asking God for forgiveness is enough.

Circumstances

Optioned expiation is applied in a number of cases, most importantly:

ONE: (Intentionally) breaking a fast in the month of Ramadan

It is expiation for intentionally breaking the fast by eating, drinking, having sexual intercourse, masturbating, or staying ritually impure due to sexual intercourse or seminal discharge (*janabah*) until dawn.[3] If a person does so intentionally and willfully, knowing the ramifications in Islamic law, expiation becomes obligatory and the person is obliged to choose the type of expiation and fulfill it.[xii]

TWO: Nullifying an obligatory period of spiritual retreat (itikaf)[xiii]

Whoever practices an obligatory period of spiritual retreat (itikaf) and then nullifies it by (1) sexual intercourse, and as an obligatory precaution, sensual activities such as touching and kissing with lust, which lead to ritual impurity (janabah) or (2) masturbation,

---

3. [Dawn means at the time of *adhan* for *fajr* prayers.—Ed.]

as an obligatory precaution, must choose the type of expiation and fulfill it.

THREE: Breaking a formal pledge (ahd)

If a person makes a formal pledge to God to do a particular act or leave off doing something but then violates the pledge, they are then obliged to choose the type of expiation and fulfill it.

Type 3

·············•◆•··············

Combined (al-Murattaba and al-Mukhayyara) Expiation

Definition

Combined expiation combines both the financial payment of feeding or clothing and the physical expiation of fasting. First, the person is obliged to pay the financial expiation, but thereafter they are free to choose between feeding or clothing ten poor people. If they are unable to do so, then they must perform the physical expiation of fasting three consecutive days.

Circumstances

Combined expiation is applied in three cases:

ONE: Expiation for swearing to leave off intercourse with one's wife (known as ilaa)

Ilaa is swearing not to have intercourse with one's wife with the intent of harming or mistreating her. Swearing to this requires paying a financial expiation of either feeding or clothing ten poor people. If he is unable to do so, then he must perform the physical expiation of fasting three consecutive days.

Two: Expiation for breaking an oath (yamin)

If a sane, free adult intentionally takes an oath to do something, invoking the name of God, or using other relevant words like *wa allahi, wa al-rahmani*, they are obliged to fulfill this oath. Breaking this oath requires paying a financial expiation of either feeding or clothing ten poor people. If they are unable to do so, then they should perform the physical expiation of fasting three consecutive days.

For some Muslims who have gotten used to swearing and invoking the name of God (or the name of the sacred house or any of the Ahl al-Bayt names) as they speak or chat without the intention of taking an oath, whatever they say has no legitimate value and therefore is not considered a pledge to God. Rather, it is considered an unpleasant practice. God said about expiation of oaths, "Allah will not impose blame upon you for what is meaningless in your oaths, but He will impose blame upon you for [breaking] what you intended of oaths. So its expiation is the feeding of ten needy people from the average of that which you feed your [own] families or clothing them or the freeing of a slave. But whoever cannot find [or afford it] — then a fast of three days [is required]. That is the expiation for oaths when you have sworn. But guard your oaths. Thus does Allah make clear to you His verses that you may be grateful" (Quran 5:89).

THREE: Expiation for breaking a vow (nadhr)

If a sane, free adult intentionally makes a vow, then they must fulfill it. To explain this further, if the *mukallaf*[4] makes it obligatory upon themselves to do some good act or to refrain from doing an act that is better not to do, for the sake or for the pleasure of God, while swearing by the name of God (Allah) and pronouncing the verbal religious formula for a vow (nadhr), then they should fulfill the vow and do what they promised. The verbal religious formula is to say, "O God, it is obligatory for me to do this or that," or to say, "O Rahman (God), I'm required to do this or that for you." Otherwise, they must choose between paying a financial expiation of either feeding or clothing ten poor people. If they are unable to do so, then they must perform the physical expiation of fasting three consecutive days.

Conditions for a valid vow

The topic of pledging or swearing a vow or nadhr is one of the common subjects in Islamic law and jurisprudence that is challenging for people and creates many questions. Thus, it is necessary to clarify the most important conditions for vows to be legitimate and valid. Otherwise, they are simply invalid and no action should be taken afterwards.

- A person who makes a vow should be (1) *baligh*—of age and therefore responsible to perform religious

---

4. A *mukallaf* is a person who is obliged to perform religious duties.

duties, (2) sane, and (3) acting with free will and clear intention. Hence, a vow by a minor (i.e., not baligh), even a minor who is *mumayyiz*,[xiv] an insane person, an intoxicated person, a person who was outraged at the moment of making the vow, or a person who had been coerced to make a vow, will not be considered legitimate.

- The vow should be possible for the person to act upon at the time of its fulfillment.

- A vow should be taken for a legitimate *halal* cause and not taken for the performance of an act that is haram or *makruh*. For example, someone makes a vow that if they go to Mecca for pilgrimage that year or visit the shrine of one of the infallibles of Ahl al-Bayt, they will become generous to the scholars. Another example could be of someone who makes a vow that if they do not stop backbiting people or stop sleeping between the time of dawn and sunrise, they will fast for a certain amount of time as a discipline.

- The vow should not violate anyone's rights. For example, it is unacceptable for a wife to make a vow of traveling away from her husband if it violates his right of sex and enjoyment.

Type 4

······◆◆······

Designated (al-Muayyana) Expiation

Definition

Designated (al-muayyana) expiation obliges a person to perform one specified act and not one of their choosing nor one that is conventionalized.

Circumstances

Someone who swears an oath by declaring (i.e., the fulfillment of which is) their disassociation from Almighty God, Prophet Muhammad (peace be upon him and his progeny), the Islamic religion, or the imams of the Ahl al-Bayt (peace be upon them) and then breaks this oath is to pay a financial expiation of feeding ten poor people.[5]

---

5. [Although the swearing of oaths is generally permissible and regularly practiced in Islam, the declaration of this type of disassociation is not permissible and is severely chastised.—Ed.]

Type 5

························◆◆◆························

Comprehensive (al-Jame) Expiation

Definition

Comprehensive (al-jame) expiation is performed by combining the expiations of fasting two consecutive months and feeding sixty poor people.

Circumstances

Comprehensive expiation happens when one intentionally kills a believer unjustly and with hostility—meaning that in addition to the financial reparation that must be paid, the intentional killer must fast two consecutive months and feed sixty poor people.

Abortion

One of the frequently encountered and common issues that causes problems today in the twenty-first century is abortion. It is a subject that falls under the title of murder. And because it has grown to become a prevalent worldwide phenomenon, it needs to be addressed in some detail here.

The prohibition of induced abortion

To start with, one must know that Islam forbids abortion, which is the intentional ending of pregnancy by removing, and thereby killing, a fetus or embryo before it can survive outside the uterus. It is not even a controversial topic in Islam because it involves killing a soul. Moreover, it is considered one of the greatest sins. God said, "Come, I will recite what your Lord has prohibited to you. [He commands] that you not associate anything with Him, and to parents, good treatment, and do not kill your children out of poverty; We will provide for you and them. And do not approach immoralities — what is apparent of them and what is concealed. And do not kill the soul which Allah has forbidden [to be killed] except by [legal] right. This has He instructed you that you may use reason" (Quran 6:151). And God has said, "if anyone killed a person not in retribution of murder, or (and) to spread mischief in the land — it would be as if he killed all mankind, and if anyone saved a life, it would be as if he saved the life of all mankind" (Quran 5:32).

Prophet Muhammad (peace be upon him and his progeny) used to accept the pledges of women after they agreed to the condition of not aborting their children. God has said, "O Prophet, when the believing women come to you pledging to you that they will not associate anything with Allah, nor will they steal, nor will they commit unlawful sexual intercourse, nor will they kill their children, nor will they bring forth a slander they have invented between their arms and legs, nor will they disobey you in what is right — then accept their pledge and ask forgiveness for them of Allah. Indeed, Allah is Forgiving and Merciful" (Quran 60:12). Moreover, God has warned anyone who disregards and belittles the value of the human soul, "Those will have lost who killed their children in foolishness without knowledge and prohibited what Allah had provided for them, inventing untruth about Allah. They have gone astray and were not [rightly] guided" (Quran 6:140).

Despite the previous facts and the opinion of Islam regarding this issue, there are two exceptions that make abortion permissible as long as the soul has not yet entered the fetus.[6] Otherwise, it would absolutely not be permissible. These two exceptions are

- if the continuation of the pregnancy significantly[7] harms the mother's health;

- if the continuation of the pregnancy puts the mother in an unbearable difficulty[8] to the extent that there is no other solution but abortion.

---

6. One sign of when the soul has entered the body is the movement of the fetus. There is no problem in using new technological devices to figure out the specific time when the soul enters the body.

7. In this situation, significant harm means extreme danger that cannot be endured during pregnancy.

8. In this situation, an example would be if the woman were to be killed because of committing adultery, where killing her for this reason is a greater immoral sin that could happen due to cultural traditions.

As for the fact that the child will be deformed or will not live for a long time after birth according to physicians or medical reports, Islam does not ever justify the termination of the pregnancy.

Questions and answers about abortion[9]

QUESTION: Sometimes doctors reach the conclusion that the fetus is afflicted with a very serious disease; it is therefore preferable that the child should be aborted for if the child were born, they would be deformed or would die soon after birth. Is it therefore permissible for the doctor to abort the fetus? Is it permissible for the mother to agree to the abortion? And who will become liable for paying the expiation of the financial reparation?

ANSWER: The fact that the child will be deformed or that they will not live for a long time after birth does not ever justify the termination of the pregnancy. Therefore, it is not permissible for the mother to consent to the abortion just as it is not permissible for the doctor to start the procedure. And the physician will become liable for the expiation of the financial reparation.

QUESTION: In recent times, thanks to modern scientific methods, physicians are able to know the situation of

---

9. These questions and answers are derived from the website of His Eminence Grand Ayatullah Ali al-Sistani (may God prolong his life).

the fetus—if it is affected by a congenital disability or not. So, if it is scientifically proven that the fetus will be deformed and affected by disabilities after birth, is it permissible to abort it?

ANSWER: The deformation of the fetus is not a justification for abortion. However, if the mother's life is in danger or the continuation of pregnancy will cause difficulty for her that is not normally bearable, and there is no other solution but abortion, only in this case, it would be permissible to abort the fetus as long as the soul has not entered into the body. If the soul has entered the body, then it is absolutely not permissible to perform the abortion.

QUESTION: If a woman became pregnant from an illegitimate source, such as rape or adultery, is it permissible for her to perform abortion? And is she required to pay the expiation of the financial reparation?

ANSWER: Abortion is permissible only before the emergence of the soul in a situation where the continuity of the pregnancy puts the mother in an unbearable difficulty to the extent that there is no other solution but abortion. The expiation of the financial reparation is then required by the one who performs the abortion. The financial reparation for abortion from adultery must be paid to the current legitimate jurist.

The amount of financial reparation (diyya) to abort the fetus

When the fetus is aborted for any of the reasons mentioned above, it is obligatory upon the one who performs the abortion to pay the financial reparation (diyya), which depends on the age of the fetus, whether male or female, according to the following details:

- Sperm stage, which is the first week of pregnancy: 487.2 grams[10] of silver[11]

- Clot stage, which is in the second and third week: 974.4 grams of silver

- Lump stage, which is from the third to the seventh week: 1461.6 grams of silver

- Bone formation stage, starting from the seventh week: 1948.8 grams of silver

- The completion of the limbs stage, starting from the eighth week: 2436 grams of silver

- Soul stage, starting from the fourth month: its financial reparation (diyya) is the same as a normal human being, which is 5250 grams of silver

---

10. The holy narrations from Ahl al-Bayt (peace be upon them) and most of the books concerned with Islamic law mention the *mithqal* as a unit of mass. The mithqal is 4.64 grams.

11. Silver could be replaced by gold depending on its material and pure form and how commonly it is used in a specific country.

Note: There is no method that can precisely identify each stage with its precise timing, as there may be an overlap between the timings of the stages of pregnancy. So, it is necessary to pay close attention when one needs to calculate and know the exact week of pregnancy.

Financial reparation (diyya) for the fetus

Financial reparation (also known as *diyya* in Arabic) is obligatory on the one who performs the abortion.

- If the mother aborts the fetus herself, it is obligatory that she pay the financial reparation to the father of the fetus.

- If the father aborts the fetus, it is obligatory that he pay the financial reparation to the mother of the fetus.

- If the fetus was aborted by a third party, such as a physician, it is obligatory that the physician pay the financial reparation to both parents of the fetus even if they requested the abortion.

Expiation for abortion

If the fetus was aborted without the involvement of any party (such as the mother, the father, or the physician) (i.e., spontaneous abortion), then there is no expiation of any sort. If the fetus was aborted mistakenly by a negligent woman who did not take good care of herself during pregnancy, then it is considered an accidental killing, which will require the previously mentioned al-murattaba expiation. However, if the abortion was planned and premeditated, then it is classified as an intentional murder, and it requires the combination of both the murattaba and the mukhayyara, which is fasting two consecutive months as well as feeding sixty poor people. This is in addition to the payment of the financial reparation depending on the age of the fetus.

Questions and answers

QUESTION: Is it permissible to use contraceptives like an intrauterine device (IUD or coil), oils, drugs, or tablets?

ANSWER: The wife may use contraceptives to prevent pregnancy, but there are a few conditions: 1) The means of contraception must stop the fertilization of the egg; it must not kill the fertilized egg. 2) The means of contraception must not cause irreparable harm to the wife, such as a disease, damage to an organ, or the transmission of an infection. 3) The insertion of the device does not involve a haram act, such as the male or female looking at the private parts of the woman's body that are forbidden for them to look at. Rather, it should be the husband who implants the intrauterine device. A physician may do it only in extreme cases as when the pregnancy threatens the wife's health.

QUESTION: Is it permissible for someone to prevent future offspring by undergoing a special surgery?

ANSWER: It is not permissible for a man or a woman to prevent future pregnancy by such means as removing her uterus or removing one or both of a man's testicles, unless the removal of such organs was required for treatment of health problems.

QUESTION: Is it permissible to temporarily prevent offspring with the potential of it becoming permanent?

ANSWER: A man may undergo a surgery to close his vasa deferentia, the ducts that convey sperm from the testicles to the urethra, and the woman may also undergo a surgery (tubal ligation) to close her fallopian tubes even if it prevents them from ever having children. However, these procedures should not involve touching or looking at the private parts of the man's or woman's body (i.e., by others) that are forbidden for them to touch or look at except in extreme cases of a threatening health situation.

Addendum

Islamic jurists have mentioned another type of expiation in Islamic laws involving expiation for hitting a child and hitting the wife. We have decided to separate them here for better clarification and organization.

Hitting a Child

Many narrations or hadiths by Ahl al-Bayt (peace be upon them) included recommendations to discipline a child, especially between seven and fourteen years of age.[12] It was reported from the Holy Prophet (peace be upon him and his family) that he said, "The right of the child upon his or her father is that the father should (1) give the child a good name, (2) discipline the child's behavior, and (3) arrange marriage for the child upon maturity." The Holy Prophet (peace and blessings be upon him and his family) has also said, "Leave the child alone for the first seven years, then discipline for the next seven years, and befriend for the seven after, otherwise leave the child alone because you have discharged your responsibility before Allah." The Prophet has also said, "The child is a master for seven years, a slave for seven years, and a minister for seven years." The words 'discipline' and 'slave' and other synonymous phrases indicate the importance and necessity of directing the child at this stage, which is the stage of adolescence—a stage at which a child begins to refine character and build future personality. During this stage, the child experiences recklessness due to their new unleashed mind, hopes and ambitions, mental and physical growth, and changes in sex hormones. Therefore, these recommendations come into play to educate the child, sometimes with firm and decisive guidance, as necessary. Other times the process of educating, disciplining, and leading them to

---

12. Shaykh al-Tabrasi, *Makarimu al-akhlaq,* p. 22 and what follows it.

the straight path might require a little force before they reach the age of Islamic puberty. At the same time though, this process is extremely dangerous as it requires wisdom and calculated behavior with full objectivity, and disciplining has to be gradual. So, parents might choose to start with recommendations and advice, and then move to motivation and encouragement, and then end with warning and admonishment. If the parents think that it is necessary, then they also might consider punishment by prevention and denial of the child's desires. After the child insists on disobedience, hitting could be considered the last level of discipline, while adhering to the following conditions:

- When the child commits a forbidden act such as stealing, lying, or harming others

- A strong belief[13] that the disciplinary process can only be effective through hitting and by no other means

- Hitting must not be because of anger or hatred.

- Hitting must not be on dangerous or sensitive organs of the body such as the head or the face but rather on the hands or legs.

- Hitting must not exceed three mild strokes.

- Hitting must not leave black, green, or red spots on the body as this will require expiation.

---

13. [A strong belief according to the father, the paternal grandfather, or an authorized person on behalf of the father—Ed.]

WHO IS ENTITLED TO DISCIPLINE?

No one has the right to discipline a child except the father or paternal grandfather or anyone who is given authority by the father to do so. In light of this, the teacher at school, the older brother, the mother, or anyone else absolutely do not have the right to hit the child unless explicit authority has been given by the father.[14]

PUNISHMENT FOR THE DISCIPLINARIAN

If the child's guardian or authorized disciplinarian exceeds their limits of hitting the child to the extent that the hitting leaves black, green, or red marks, then the legitimate jurist is allowed to impose a punishment on them. The punishment depends on how hard the hitting was and the color it leaves on the child's skin (i.e., the extent of harm). An alternative could be that the disciplinarian asks the child for forgiveness when he reaches adulthood.

Hitting a Wife

Having a strong family is based on respecting the rights and duties of others on the basis of

- human dignity ("And We have certainly honored the children of Adam." Quran 17:70);

---

14. There are numerous factors (as stated above) and stipulations concerning this issue.

- tranquility, love, and compassion ("And of His signs is that He created for you from yourselves mates that you may find tranquility in them; and He placed between you affection and mercy. Indeed in that are the signs for a people who give thought." 30:21);

- living with kindness ("And live with them in kindness." 4:19);

- living as an integrated whole ("They are clothing (cover) for you and you are clothing (cover) for them" 2:187).

The Islamic family depends on such a foundation and gains sanctity and special reverence to the extent that it was narrated that Prophet Muhammad (peace be upon him and his progeny) said, "No house is built in Islam more loved by God than [the house of] marriage."[15]

This sacred house needs trusses that support its structure, strengthen it, and harden it against the cracks that occur during day-to-day challenges fighting the difficulties of life. Among these dangerous difficulties and tribulations, we find that private affairs between husband and wife are the most challenging because they cannot always be revealed to others even when seeking help or support. Therefore, they (the husband and wife) are the only ones who have the ability to carry out the reconciliation process to repair their marriage. This reconciliation and reformation

---

15. Al-Hurr al-Amili, *Tafsilu wasaili al-Shia,* vol. 14, p. 3.

process may be difficult and arduous, and indeed it requires the fear of God, particularly sometimes if, in the heat of emotions and anger, it results in the man having hit the wife.[16]

THE AMOUNT OF FINANCIAL REPARATION (DIYYA)

The amount of financial reparation for hitting the wife or any other human being (to the extent that the hitting leaves a mark) becomes obligatory and its amount depends on the impact and level of harm. If the hitting was

- on the face and has led to
  - blackness, the diyya is 20.9 grams of gold;[17]
  - greenness, the diyya is 10.4 grams of gold;
  - redness, the diyya is 5.2 grams of gold.
- on any other part of the body resulting in
  - blackness, the diyya is 10.4 grams of gold;
  - greenness, the diyya is 5.2 grams of gold;
  - redness, the diyya is 2.6 grams of gold.

---

16. The conditions and factors related to this issue are numerous and complex, and thus, they are beyond the scope of this booklet. Please consult imam-us.org for further details.

17. The gold depends on its material and pure form and how common its usage is in a specific country.

How to
Perform Expiation

It is permissible to choose between providing poor people a meal to eat until they are full or just delivering them the food. The minimum amount of a meal one should give is equivalent to 1.65 pounds of wheat[18] and, as an obligatory precaution, double the amount.

It is permissible to divide sixty meals into two categories—the first given to the poor until they are full; the second delivered to them so that they take care of it themselves.

If poor people are children, the amount of food supply given should be the same as the adult. However, if they were given food to eat until they were full, then one must consider two children the equivalent of one adult (i.e., it will not suffice to give a child's portion size to an adult).

The person fulfills the expiation responsibility as soon as the food is delivered to the poor people. In other words, the person does not have to make sure the poor

---

18. In the old tradition of weighing units, it was called *al-mudd*, which is equivalent to 750 grams.

people eat the food. The poor people may do whatever they wish with the food—like sell it or give it to others.

It is not permissible to feed only one poor person sixty meals. Nor is it permissible to give sixty meals to fewer than sixty poor people—such as giving thirty meals to thirty poor people twice a day.

You may feed sixty poor people at different times of the year and in different places. So, for example, ten of them are fed in the month of Rajab in Najaf, twenty are fed in the month of Sha'ban in Karbala, and thirty are fed in the month of Ramadan in Samarra in the same year or in another year.

The obligatory clothing for one poor person is what is commonly worn, and it is recommended (mustahabb) to give two [articles of clothing].

There is no difference between clothing a child or an adult, unless the child is very young, such as an infant, as an obligatory precaution.

It is not permissible to give a man's clothes to a woman nor is it permissible to give a woman's clothes to a man. Nor is it permissible to give children's clothing to an adult or vice versa.

It is obligatory that in murattaba expiation the kaffarah be one type. For example, it is not permissible for someone who intentionally breaks a fast in the month of

Ramadan to fast thirty days and feed thirty poor people—it has to be either one or the other but not both.

Expiation is obligatory on all individuals who are involved in a given act of murder, whether it was intentional or by mistake.

It is not permissible to delay the payment of expiation due to procrastination and/or laziness. However, it is permissible to delay the payment of expiation for reasonable reasons when, for example, the money is needed in other regions or perhaps to ensure its safe delivery.

It is permissible to pay money instead of paying expiation of food

- to a reliable person who can be trusted to ensure that the money of expiation has been spent on food;
- to a reliable person who, at the same time, is one of the poor (i.e., poor themselves).

It is obligatory to observe the other conditions of performing religious expiation. For example:

- It is necessary to perform the fasting for two consecutive months without interruption even if the person had to connect the thirtieth day of the first month to the first day of the second month. The person then may choose to disperse the remaining days for the second month as desired.

- The cause of interrupting the fasting for reasons such as traveling or having menstruation or postnatal bleeding must not affect the consecutiveness of the fasting. So, if the interrupting factor started on the fifth day of the month and ended on the tenth day, the person is obliged to continue fasting the eleventh day as if it was the sixth day.

A person should restart expiation of fasting if they knew that the fast would be inevitably separated by *Eid al-Adha*, for example, or the month of Ramadan.

The ability, possibility, and the potential to perform expiation should be based on the time it is performed, not the time it becomes obligatory. So, if a person were obliged to fast two consecutive months and something prevented them from fasting, such as traveling or a health condition, they must perform fasting at a later time but with no additional penalty. Or, if they had to feed sixty poor people and did not have enough money at the time and they know that after a month or two they will be able to pay expiation, then they can do it when they get the money as long as they do not neglect it.

It is not permissible to pay expiation on behalf of someone else as a form of a donation without their request or permission even if they were not able to perform it themselves. However, it is permissible to do that on behalf of the dead.

It is not obligatory for the heirs to perform expiation on behalf of the dead unless requested to do so in a will. If it was requested in the will, then it should be paid from the one-third that the deceased has personal discretion over, but if the amount was greater than the one-third, then it depends on the satisfaction of the heirs and their decision.

When a person is unable to perform expiation of fasting, feeding, or clothing, even for a small amount, they must then beg God for pardon and ask Him for forgiveness.

To Whom Expiation Is Paid

The required conditions in paying expiation are as follows:

It must be paid to the needy/destitute (*miskin*) and the poor (*faqir*).

- The needy is the person who cannot afford their daily food.
- The poor is the person who cannot support their annual food/expenses for the lack of resources and power.
  - Lack of resources means they do not have enough money to buy what they need, including shelter, food, and clothes throughout the year.
  - Lack of power means they cannot gain money from an investment, trading, a job, or any other type of work.

The one who deserves the money must be a Muslim[xv] and, as an obligatory precaution, a believer *(mumin).*[19]

---

19. A believer (*mumin*) is a person who believes in the twelve imams being the successors of Prophet Muhammad (peace and blessing be upon all of them).

Epilogue

We introduced this booklet by explaining how expiation, or kaffarah, in Islam is a system of discipline. This system has a profound educational and spiritual impact on a human being whose ultimate goal is to seek perfection in this life. The religion of Islam has expanded the field of education and development to the point of teaching humans to stay away from committing sins. It clarifies how one can stay away from wrongful acts (that will eventually require the performance of expiation) with the objective of providing an appropriate spiritual and moral atmosphere.

If a human being falters and becomes prey to the social (non-Islamic) pressures that would draw them to behaviors that may require expiation, Islam intervenes and imposes certain recommended expiation (*kaffarat mustahabba*) and other atonement, which are preferred and favored by Islamic jurists. These include but are not limited to the following:

expiation for someone in a position of power (a *sultan*)	to provide the needs of their people
expiation for backbiting	to ask forgiveness from the one who was backbit

expiation for a missed evening prayer	to fast the next day
expiation for sitting with bad company	To say as you stand up, "Glorified be your Lord, the Lord of Honor and Power! (He is free) from what they attribute unto Him. And peace be on the messengers. And all the praise and thanks be to Allah, Lord of the Worlds."
expiation for laughing in offense of others	to say, "God, do not dislike me"
expiation for ornithomancy (the practice of reading omens from the actions of birds) or other such divinations	to put your trust in God

Notes

Preface

i. [Puberty in the Islamic sense (*baligh*) means that a person has reached the age at which they are religiously duty-bound. Although there are specific physical signs that indicate a person has reached the age of being baligh, jurists generally agree it occurs when a girl has completed nine lunar years and a boy fifteen lunar years.—Ed.]

Introduction

ii. Other limits include those for intentional murder or falsely accusing someone of intentionally doing something wrong (*qadhf*), but these can be absolved respectively if the victim's family or the person who was falsely accused gives a pardon.

iii. Islamic penalty code that requires that the victim or the family of the victim (if deceased) have the right of equal and proportional reprisal as a requisite for justice.

iv. The legitimate jurist is a scholar who specializes in Islamic jurisprudence and has reached the degree of diligence in deriving and developing Islamic laws from their original sources (Quran and hadith) and has been characterized by a set of certain qualities particularly devotion, loyalty, and superior knowledge amongst other jurists at the time.

v. [In English too, the prefix 'ex' means "out of" or "from," so expiation has to do with removing something or taking something away. In religious terms, whether in the Holy Quran or the Bible, it has to do with taking away guilt through the payment of a penalty or the offering of expiation.—Trans.]

vi. Refer to *Lisan al-Arab* by Ibn Mandoor and encyclopedias and books of jurisprudence like *Al-kafi* and *Al-tahdib*.

vii. [To explain this further, the idea lies behind paying some amount to redress an imbalance or to compensate for performing a sinful act (i.e., a kind of punishment or penalty). This penalty or expiation is defined by Islamic laws in accordance with the type of shortfall or sin; it may take the form of financial penalty, such as feeding a specific number of poor people, or clothing them; it could be personal, such as fasting and abstaining from some of life's necessities and luxuries.—Trans.]

Pre-ordained (al-Murattaba) Expiation

viii. [The rules of *qudra* and *istita* relating to a person's physical state and ability to carry out the act are specifically described in Islamic jurisprudence. Please consult additional sources for more information.—Ed.]

ix. One of the standard modes of expiation in Islam is to free a slave. Through this form of atonement, Islam was able to virtually eliminate the slave trade and the enslavement of the poor by the rich. As a result, slavery is not commonly practiced openly in our societies, nor is it socially or legally acceptable. Therefore, it would be difficult for a person to apply this type of expiation now and it has not been included.

x. The phrase "obligatory precaution" (*ihtiyat wajib*) is a precaution from the jurist in the edict. Thus, the follower may either act on this precaution or act on the *fatwa* of the second most knowledgeable and current jurist.

xi. Including "*dhihar* between a husband and wife," which will not be mentioned in this booklet because it is a condition that is no longer common in our contemporary era. [In pre-Islamic times, this practice of a husband telling a wife that she was like the back of his mother was not uncommon.—Ed.]

Optioned (al-Mukhayyara) Expiation

xii. The difference between expiation (*kaffarah*) and ransom (*fidyah*): Fidyah is a form of compensation for what a person has broken of fast due to illness, pregnancy, or travel during the month of Ramadan and could not make up (do *qada*) before the beginning of the next month of Ramadan. In this case, one is required to give fidyah, and it is feeding one poor person, in which at least 1.65 lb.

of common food (e.g., wheat or rice) should be given, and the person must make up the missed fast too.

xiii.   *Itikaf* (the spiritual retreat) is a form of recommended (mustahabb) worship during which a person stays in a mosque for a particular time period (especially the last ten nights of the month of Ramadan) worshipping God while maintaining certain conditions. This spiritual retreat can be obligatory in a vow or an oath that one takes on oneself.

Combined (al-Murattaba and al-Mukhayyara) Expiation

xiv.   A *mumayyiz* is a child who is near the age of a *baligh.* They are capable of rational actions and knowing the difference between *haram* and *halal.* Some of their religious duties are accepted by God, like following a jurist, undertaking something, and buying and selling.

To Whom Expiation Is Paid

xv.   It is no secret that the financial system of worship in Islam is very wide, and it can accommodate every poor Muslim or non-Muslim alike as in the public house of charity. However, there are restrictions and special conditions for some of its sections, including expiation sections.

Glossary

ahd (عهد). Formal pledge

baligh (بالغ). Puberty in the Islamic sense means that a person has reached the age at which they are religiously duty-bound. Although there are specific physical signs that indicate a person has reached the age of being baligh, jurists generally agree it occurs when a girl has completed nine lunar years and a boy fifteen lunar years.

dhihar (ظهار). The practice of declaring that a man's wife is as his mother's back to him. This occurred primarily in pre-Islamic times.

diyya (دية). Financial reparation

Eid al-Adha (عيد الاضحى). "Feast of Sacrifice" commemorating Prophet Ibrahim's willingness to sacrifice his son out of obedience to God

faqir (فقير). The poor person who cannot support their annual (i.e., one year) food/expenses for the lack of resources and power
- Lack of resources means they do not have enough money to buy what they need, including shelter, food, and clothes throughout the year.
- Lack of power means they cannot gain money from an investment, trading, a job, or any other type of work.

fatwa (فتوى). A religious edict

fidyah (فدية). A form of compensation for what a person
has broken of fast due to illness, pregnancy, or
travel during the month of Ramadan and could
not make up (do qada) before the beginning of the
next month of Ramadan.

fiqh (فقه). Islamic jurisprudence

fitna (فتنة). Trial

hadith (*pl. ahadith*)(حديث/أحاديث). Sayings of the
Prophet (pbuh) and the imams (p)

halal (حلال). A jurisprudential term meaning
permissible under Islamic law

haram (حرام). A jurisprudential term meaning
forbidden under Islamic law

hudud (حدود). The known, recognized, and explicitly
mentioned limits set by God the pardon for which
rests with Him

ihtiyat wajib; ihtiyat wujubi (إحتياط واجب / إحتياط وجوبي).
Precautionary obligation. This means a
precautionary measure in which the follower
must either follow the opinion of their jurist or
follow the opinion of the second-most learned
jurist on that issue.

ilaa (الايلاء). Swearing to leave off intercourse with
one's wife

istighfar (استغفار). To ask forgiveness from God

itikaf (اعتكاف). Spiritual retreat. A form of
recommended act of worship during which a
person stays in a mosque for a particular time
period (especially the last ten nights of the month

of Ramadan) worshipping God while maintaining certain conditions.

jame (جمع). Comprehensive

janabah (جنابة). The state of impurity caused by discharge of semen or sexual intercourse

kaffarah (pl. *kaffarat*)(كفارة). The religious penalty to absolve a sin. Paying some amount to redress an imbalance or to compensate for performing a sinful act (i.e., a kind of punishment or penalty). This penalty or expiation/atonement is defined by Islamic laws in accordance with the type of shortfall or sin; it may take the form of financial penalty, such as feeding a specific number of poor people, or clothing them; it could be personal, such as fasting and abstaining from some of life's necessities and luxuries.

legitimate jurist (مجتهد) The legitimate jurist is a scholar who specializes in Islamic jurisprudence and has reached the degree of diligence in deriving and developing Islamic laws from their original sources (Quran and hadith) and has been characterized by a set of certain qualities particularly devotion, loyalty, and superior knowledge amongst other jurists at the time.

makruh (مكروه). A jurisprudential term meaning detestable or abominable. Although such acts are not forbidden or subject to punishment, a person who abstains from such acts will be rewarded.

miskin (مسكين). A needy/destitute person who cannot afford their daily food/expenses

mithqal al-sayrafi (المثقال الصيرفي). A weight that is well-known in the market; especially to the goldsmith (.16 ounce/4.64 grams)

muayyana (المعيَّنة). Designated expiation

mukallaf (مكلف). Person who is obliged to perform religious duties

mukhayyara (الْمُخَيَّرَة). Optioned expiation

mumayyiz (مميز). A child who is near the age of a baligh. They are capable of rational actions and knowing the difference between haram and halal. Some of their religious duties are accepted by God, like following a jurist, undertaking something, and buying and selling.

mumin (مؤمن). A Muslim person who believes in the twelve imams being the successors of Prophet Muhammad (peace and blessings be upon all of them)

murattaba (مرتبة). Pre-ordained expiation

mustahabb (مستحب). A jurisprudential term meaning recommended under Islamic law. It is better to perform recommended actions than not to perform them, but they are not compulsory.

nadhr (نذر). Formal vow

qada (قضاء). Fulfillment of lapsed/missed religious duty

qadhf (قذف). Falsely accusing someone of intentionally doing something wrong

qisas (قصاص). Retribution. Islamic penalty code that requires that the victim or the family of the victim (if deceased) have the right of equal and proportional reprisal as a requisite for justice.

tazirat (تعزيرات). Judicial sentences

yamin (يمين). Oath

zawal (زوال). Midday. The time of the noon prayer when the sun crosses the meridian. It changes during the different times of year depending on the length of day and night.

Other publications from I.M.A.M.

Available for purchase online

❖ Fasting: A Haven from Hellfire
   by Grand Ayatullah al-Sayyid Ali al-Sistani

❖ Youth: Advice from Grand Ayatullah
   al-Sayyid Ali al-Sistani

❖ The Illuminating Lantern: An Exposition of
   Subtleties from the Quran
   by Shaykh Habib al-Kadhimi

❖ God's Emissaries: Adam to Jesus
   by Shaykh Rizwan Arastu

❖ Tajwid: A Guide to Qur'anic Recitation
   by Shaykh Rizwan Arastu

❖ Who Is Hussain?
   by Dr. Mehdi Saeed Hazari

❖ Shia Muslims: Our Identity, Our Vision, and the
   Way Forward
   by Sayyid M. B. Kashmiri